MW00977031

**RAINBOW
STUDIES
INTERNATIONAL**

A Special Gift

Presented to

Helen & Arline

From

Debra & Joel

On the Occasion of

Friendship

Date

2 - 12 - 1999

Gifts of Love™

"Gifts of Hope™" Series

Compiled by Billy & Janice Hughey

RAINBOW STUDIES INTERNATIONAL

Creating Colorful Treasures™

Gifts of Love ™

from the "Gifts of Hope™" Series
Copyright © 1997 by Rainbow Studies, Inc.
All rights reserved.

Published by: Rainbow Studies International, P.O. Box 759, El Reno, OK 73036

THE RAINBOW STUDY BIBLE®
Copyright © 1981, 1986, 1989, 1992, 1995 and 1996
by Rainbow Studies, Inc. All rights reserved.

Color Coding System, Bold Line® Words of Trinity System,
Book Outlines and Sectional Headings.
Copyright © 1981, 1986, 1989, 1992, 1995 and 1996
by Rainbow Studies, Inc. All rights reserved.

Scripture taken from the HOLY BIBLE: NEW INTERNATIONAL VERSION®. NIV®
Copyright © 1973, 1978 and 1984
by International Bible Society.
Used by permission of Zondervan Publishing House.

The "NIV" and "New International Version" trademarks are registered in the United States Patent and
Trademark Office by International Bible Society.

Verses marked (TLB) are taken from The Living Bible © 1971.
Used by permission of Tyndale House Publishers, Inc., Wheaton, IL 60189. All rights reserved.

Design Concept by Rainbow Studies International and Design Life Studio.

ISBN 0-933657-56-0

Library of Congress Catalog Card Number 97-76614

1 2 3 4 5 6 7 8 9 - 01 00 99 98 97
Rainbow Studies International, El Reno, Oklahoma 73036, U.S.A.

Printed in the United States of America

The "LOVE" Themes

LOVE ~ JOY ~ KINDNESS

MERCY ~ MOURNING ~ LAMENT

COMFORT ~ COMPASSION ~ PEACE

SYMPATHY ~ HUMILITY ~ CHARITY

"Just as I am, God loves me."

LOVE

To Love

is

to make

of one's

heart a

swinging

door.

Howard Thurman

Many waters cannot quench love;
rivers cannot wash it away.
If one were to give all the wealth
of his house for love,
it would be utterly scorned.

Song of Songs 8:7 NIV

*Love doesn't make
the world go round.
Love is what* **makes**
the ride **worthwhile**.

Franklin P. Jones

*Who, being LOVED,
is poor?*

Oscar Wilde

LOVE

*I have a very strong feeling
that the opposite of love is not hate —
it's apathy.*

Leo Buscaglia

*It is better to have loved
and lost,
than not to love at all.*

Alfred, Lord Tennyson

The loneliest
place
in the world
is the
human heart
when
love *is absent.*

E. C. McKenzie

LOVE

Does God love us

because we are special —

or are we

special

because God loves us?

William Arthur Ward

LOVE

LOVE and a cough
cannot be hid.

George Herbert

What the world really needs
is more *LOVE* and less paperwork.

Pearl Bailey

LOVE

I am not one of those who do not
believe in love at first sight,
but I believe in taking a second look.

Henry Vincent

Love is not a feeling but a choice.

Soren Kierkegaard

Love is a deep well

from which
you may
drink
often,

but into
which you
may fall
but once.

Ellye Howell Glover

It is not our toughness

that keeps us

warm at night,

but our tenderness

which makes others

want to keep us warm.

Harold Lyon

Love *does not consist in gazing at each other,*
but in looking outward **together**
in the same direction.

Antoine de Saint-Exupéry

In real love *you want the other person's good.*
In romantic love you want the other person.

Margaret Anderson

The bee is more honored

than other animals,

not because she labors,

but BECAUSE she labors for others.

St. John Chrysostom

CHARITY

No person was ever honored for what he received.
Honor has been the reward for what he gave.

Calvin Coolidge

*It is more blessed **to give** than to receive.*

Acts 20:35 KJV

Consideration

for others can mean

taking a wing

instead of a drumstick.

Garth Henrichs

It's not true that nice guys finish last.
Nice guys *are winners*
before the game even starts.

Addison Walker

Do to others as you
would have them do to you.

Luke 6:31 NIV

Be **kind**, *for every one you meet*
is fighting a battle.

John Watson

You cannot do a kindness *too soon,*
for you never know how soon it will be too late.

Ralph Waldo Emerson

One kind word

can **warm**

three winter months.

Japanese Proverb

KINDNESS

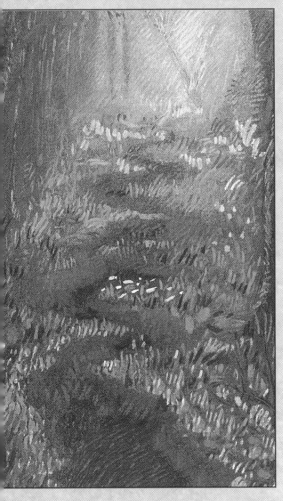

I expect to pass
through life but once.
If therefore, there be any
kindness I can show,
or any good thing
I can do
to any fellow being,
let me do it now,
and not defer or neglect it,
as I shall not pass
this way again.

William Penn

KINDNESS

*I am leaving you
with a **gift** —
peace of mind and heart!
And the peace I give
isn't fragile
like the peace
the world gives.*

John 14:27 TJB

PEACE

They want

PEACE,

but they want a

GUN to help

get it with.

Will Rogers

PEACE

*The mere absence of war
is not* **peace**.

John F. Kennedy

Where there is peace, **God** *is.*

George Herbert

The wolf will live with the lamb,
the leopard will lie down with the goat,

the calf and the lion and the yearling together;
and a little child will lead them.

Isaiah 11:6 NIV

PEACE

When things are bad,
we take comfort in the thought
that they could always be worse.
And when they are,
we find hope in the thought
that things are so bad
they have to get better.

Malcolm S. Forbes

*One reason a dog can be such a comfort
when you're* **feeling blue**
is that he doesn't try to find out why.

Anonymous

Most of our comforts
grow up
between **our crosses**.

Edward Young

As a mother comforts her child,
so will I comfort you . . . .

Isaiah 66:13 NIV

There is no Greater
loan than a sympathetic ear

Frank Tyger

Sympathy is your pain in my heart.

Halford E. Luccock

Even the little pigs grunt
when the old boar suffers.

Selma Lagerlöf

COMPASSION

*Anyone can sympathize with the sufferings
of a friend, but it requires a very fine
nature to sympathize with a friend's success.*

Oscar Wilde

REJOICE *with them that do rejoice,
and weep with them that* **weep***.*

Romans 12:15 KJV

If you're going to care about the fall of the sparrow you can't pick and choose who's going to be the sparrow.

Madeleine L'Engle

Somewhere over the rainbow
Bluebirds fly.
Birds fly over the rainbow —
Why then, oh why can't I?

Edgar Y. Harburg

It is often hard to bear the tears
that we ourselves have caused.

Marcel Proust

Oh, my anguish, my anguish! I writhe in pain.
Oh, the agony of my heart!
My heart pounds within me, I cannot keep silent.

Jeremiah 4:19 NIV

LAMENT

Of all the sad
words
*of tongue or **pen**,*
the saddest are these:
"It might have been."

John Greenleaf Whittier

The **soul** would have no

raimbow

had the eyes no **tears**.

John Vance Cheney

Tears are often the telescope
by which men see far into heaven.

Henry Ward Beecher

In the real dark
night of the
soul
it is always
three o'clock
in the morning.

E. Scott Fitzgerald

Sorrow is a fruit:

God does not make it grow on limbs

too weak to bear it.

Hugo

Believe me,
every man has his
secret sorrow,
which the world knows not;
and oftentimes
we call a man cold
when he is only sad.

Henry Wadsworth Longfellow

COMPASSION

Now I know
I've got a **HEART**,
'cause it's BREAKING.

The Tin Man
(The Wizard of Oz)

The Lord is close to those whose hearts are breaking . . . .

Psalm 34:18 TJB

*They wept until
they could weep no more.*

1 Samuel 30:4 TJB

Rich tears!

*What power lies in those
falling drops.*

Mary Delarivier Manley

*Who would recognize the unhappy
if* **grief** *had no language?*

Publilius Syrus

*Take my word for it, the saddest thing
under the sky is a soul incapable of sadness.*

Countess de Gasparin

The dew of compassion is a tear.

George Gordon Byron

On the *sands of life*
sorrow treads heavily,
and leaves a print
time cannot wash away.

Henry Neele

I cannot prevent the **birds of sorrow**
from passing over my head,
but I can keep them
from building a nest in my hair.

Chinese Proverb

Do not rejoice at my **grief**,
for when mine is old, yours will be new.

Spanish Proverb

Noble deeds and hot baths
are the best cures
for depression.

Dodie Smith

When I'm sad
I sing,
and then others
can be sad
with me.

Mark Twain

Happiness
makes up in
H
E
I
G
H
T
for what it lacks in
LENGTH.

Robert Frost

No matter how dull, or how mean,

or how wise a man is,

he feels that happiness

is his indisputable right.

Helen Keller

Most people are about as happy

as they make up their minds to be.

Abraham Lincoln

Enjoy
the little things,
for one day
you may
look back and
realize they were
the BIG things.

Robert Brault

JOY

LAUGHTER is

the shortest

distance

between two

people.

Victor Borge

Laughter is a tranquilizer
with no side effects.

Arnold H. Glasow

He

who LAUGHS,

LASTS*!*

Mary Pettibone Poole

A laugh is a

smile

that

BURSTS.

Mary H. Waldrip

The boy on the sandlot gets

just as big a kick out of a

home run *as Babe Ruth.*

Will Rogers

After being asked if football
coach Tom Landry ever smiles,
former player Walt Garrison
replied, "I don't know.
I only played there nine years."

JOY

It's good sportsmanship
to not pick up lost golf balls
while they are still rolling.

Mark Twain

KINDNESS

HAPPINESS
is an
INSIDE
job.

Anonymous

If you have no **joy** *in your religion,*
there's a leak *in your Christianity somewhere.*

Billy Sunday

Joy *is the* ECHO
of God's life within us.

Joseph Marmion

There is joy

in the presence of the angels *of God*

over one sinner that repenteth.

Luke 15:10 KJV

HAPPINESS

is good health

and a bad memory.

Ingrid Bergman

Now and then it's good

to pause in our

pursuit of happiness

and just

be happy.

Anonymous

HAPPINESS *is perfume,*

you can't pour it

on somebody else

without getting

a few drops

on yourself.

James Van Der Zee

The **fragrance**

always remains

in the hand

that *gives* the

rose.

Heda Bejar

In Faith and Hope the world will disagree,
But all mankind's concern is Charity.

Alexander Pope

If you haven't any charity in your heart,
you have the worst kind of heart trouble.

Bob Hope

Lots of people
think they are charitable
if they give away their old clothes
and things they don't want.

Myrtle Reed

CHARITY

That which you cannot give away,

you do not possess.

It possesses you.

Ivern Ball

If CHARITY *cost no money*

and BENEVOLENCE

caused no heartache,

the world would be

full of PHILANTHROPISTS.

Yiddish Proverb

HOSPITALITY

consists in a little fire,

a little food,

and an immense quiet.

Ralph Waldo Emerson

After that, he poured water into a basin

and began to wash his disciples' feet,

drying them with the towel

that was wrapped around him.

John 13:5 NIV

HUMILITY

Let me fall into the hands
of the LORD,
for his MERCY *is very great;*
but do not let me fall
into the hands of men.

1 Chronicles 21:13 NIV

To err is human, to forgive, divine.

Alexander Pope

Forgiveness
is the fragrance
the violet sheds
on the heel that has crushed it.

Mark Twain

Those who
travel
the **high road**
of humility

are not troubled
by heavy traffic.

Alan K. Simpson

*The really tough thing
about true humility
is you can't brag
about it.*

Gene Brown

Don't be humble. You're not that great.

Golda Meir

Sometimes
I AMAZE
myself.
I say this
HUMBLY.

Don King

Nothing is as hard to do gracefully
as getting down off your high horse.

Franklin P. Jones

The sufficiency of my merit is to know
that my merit is not sufficient.

St. Augustine

Give the gift that shows that special someone
how much you care!

Other "Gifts of Hope™" Series Selections

GIFT BOOK   ❧ *Gifts of Faith*™

GIFT BOOK   ❧ *Gifts for the Family*™

GIFT BOOK   ❧ *Gifts for Life's Journey*™

❧ *Perpetual Calendar*

❧ *Blank Journal*

Available at fine bookstores nationwide
or call 1-800-242-5348

RAINBOW
STUDIES
INTERNATIONAL

Creating Colorful Treasures™

Give the gift that shows that special someone how much you care!

Additional Rainbow Studies Products

❧ *A Rainbow of Hope*™

❧ *The Rainbow Study Bible*®

- *New International Version* • *King James Version*
- *The Living Bible* • *Reina-Valera Revisión 1960, Spanish*
- *Portuguese*

❧ *CD-ROM – The Rainbow Study Bible*® –
  Parallel Versions by RainbowSoft™

- *New International Version* • *King James Version*
- *Reina-Valera Revisión 1960, Spanish*

❧ *"In The Beginning" Children's Video Collection*

  51 Animated Biblical Stories of the Old & New Testaments.
  Available in English or Spanish.

Available at fine bookstores nationwide
or call 1-800-242-5348